The Aura

DAN OLT

PAGE PUBLISHING, INC.
New York, NY

First originally published by Page Publishing, Inc. 2017

ISBN 978-1-64082-826-1 (Paperback)
ISBN 978-1-64082-827-8 (Digital)

Printed in the United States of America

It was a warm, pleasant afternoon in Chicago, and the northeast wind blowing off the lake brought negative ions to give the city a touch of euphoria. Chad pulled into the parking lot of a hamburger chili place he ate at when one has a taste for something spicy and feels like taking a little risk.

He sat himself down in one of the small booths and got some quick service as usual, ordering two chili dogs with fries. He didn't buy the newspaper today, so he timidly glanced out the window and around the restaurant. Even though he worked at not letting his glances turn into stares, he still, sometimes, got a questioning look or back-off comment. He saw a guy sitting at the counter that rightfully looked familiar. Yeah, Matt Cotz. He hadn't seen him, it must be eight to ten years.

He took out a piece of notepaper and wrote down the following: *caffeine kid, sportsman park.* That should bring old Matt back a memory or two. We were in our late teens at Sportsman's Park Racetrack and Matt had $50 to win on caffeine kid, and he won at decent odds.

When the waitress returned with his food, Chet handed her the note to give to Matt. Reading the note, a wide grin came to his face which doubled as he turned his head and saw his friend Chad. He then joined him at the booth. Since it was during Matt's lunch break, the two talked just briefly and exchanged phone numbers. Matt worked at a local trucking firm as a spotter.

Chad has been working as a security guard for the Baani Corporation. He questioned whether he became a security guard by choice or because his energy level began to wane about ten years ago.

A few months ago, after a little persuasion by a relative, Chad went in for physical exam. A very observant MD found that he had an underactive thyroid, a progressive illness that may have started twenty years ago. The discovery of this is what changed Chad's life, is the basis of Chad's life, and is the basis for much of the following story.

For the most part, his life was moving along normally until he was about twenty-five years old. Before that, he spent two years in the military, including a tour in Vietnam. He then went to a junior college and received an AA degree in liberal arts. He also worked in machine shops when necessary. Gradually, unknowing of the cause, he lost much of his physical and mental drive due to his thyroid condition. He also lost twenty pounds just before his physical exam.

So after some medication, etc., he never felt so good in his entire forty-five years of life. With this newly acquired zest, there were so many things he wanted to do. One area he could really measure the increase of his vitality was how effortlessly he swam now. What he wasn't exactly crazy about was being a security guard and the wages that went with the job.

A short while after starting this job, he was given a casual interview. At that time, his lack of aggression and ambition is what the corporation liked about him. After the interview, he was offered and he accepted the duty of taking a flight every six months or so to Pakistan. On this trip, he would return with two drums of fragrance oil, which was used in the manufacturing of perfumes, etc.

For this, he was given $500 for each trip along with weeks' regular salary. He thought the $500 was not a bad bonus for what he almost considered a vacation. Later, when he discovered each shipment had an average value of 1.5 million, he didn't see the $500 in quite the same way.

For the most part, Chad always considered himself to be on the side of good morals. He questioned himself on why he was going to steal a shipment of fragrance oils he was supposed to deliver. His thoughts on why were (1) he was bored and wanted some excitement, (2) he now had added energy and zest for life, (3) the desire for a change in lifestyle would call for more money. He concluded, "Hey, why not? Baani had plenty of money."

Baani Corporation manufactured various products, such as shampoos, deodorants, and bubble baths. It also made some of the finest perfumes and colognes that, through centuries of development, could guarantee sexual arousal in almost anyone.

In a few days, Matt's phone rings.

"Yeah, hello, Matt? What ya say we hit a ball game tomorrow night?"

"Yeah, sure," Matt says.

"Okay, I'll pick ya up about seven. Let me have your address."

During their talk at the restaurant the other day, Matt stated he had recently gotten divorced. He was now living in a one-bedroom apartment in a complex on the south side of Chicago.

Chet rang the bell and went back to the car and waited for Matt to come down. Matt got in the car. There was a moment of silence. Matt then said with a little emotion as possible, "Yeah, I'm divorced now!" He pointed to a late-model compact car and said, "My clothes are what I got out of it. She got the house, the kids, new station wagon and some money we had saved. That's the way I really want it for her and the kids to have it good. Just one of those things he said. Spoken in a way that was new to me, as a soft-hearted real-dad type of guy and that was where we left it."

While driving to the ballpark, Chet said, "Matt, remember when we were younger, how you and I would talk about pulling a job of some sort? Well, if you're still game for something like that, I think I found it." Matt, cool and calm, said, "I'm listening."

As they arrived at the midst of Sox fans heading for their seats, there was a medium-sized turnout with some empty areas, and Matt and Chad chose one of them. Here, they could continue what was started in the car. As they sat down, the beer man promptly arrived and a sale of two was made. Matt didn't wait too long before saying tell me more and then took a drink from his headed cup of beer, a cloud of optimism was in the air.

"Man, as I told you the other day, I work as security for a company named Baani. They make shampoo, perfumes, stuff like that. Every six months or so, I fly over to Pakistan and bring back about a hundred gallons of these fragrance oils they use in the products they make. It's more like a vacation than anything. I stay about a week on this large flower plantation. I'm treated like a king. It makes them happy when I come over since each deal is worth roughly $1.5 million. That's right. I said 1.5 million for a hundred gallons of this stuff.

"Well, anyway, about a year ago, a guy hands me a letter with an offer to buy a load for a whopping $750 grand with an address and phone number where he can be reached in New Delhi. That's a stop-off point I make on my way back to the States. That's where you come in. I figure the best place for us to skip out with the oil would be the airport just outside New Delhi. Yeah, a small plane takes me there from the plantation.

"There, instead of boarding the usual 747 back to the United States. You'll be waiting with a van. We then take the load to meet the buyer. I do carry on these trips. I'm guessing he won't try anything funny. You never can tell though. So keep in mind we're going to have to be on our toes. None of this rattles you, does it, buddy?"

Matt, with a mostly clear-sounding voice, said no. Matt then asks a very important question. "What happens if we get caught?"

Chad answered, "I figure the most, a couple of years or, with a sharp lawyer, just probation. I don't really have any strikes against me. You don't either, do ya?" Matt says no.

Time at the ballpark was passing quickly, and the White Sox were winning. Chet called out to the beer vendor. Then the two sat quietly, paying attention to the game between thoughts of the conversation that took place.

As he ate his cornflakes, a simple kind of guy he thought about all the plans he had made—about Baani and the great and exciting life he was going to have after the hard part was over. It was just like what the MD told him it would be. He felt his thyroid gland working in full swing now. He had a physical and mental strength like never before. To validate this change was a thirty pin increase in his bowling average and how effortless he found swimming to be now.

The MD gave him a warning not to let this eagerness get out of control. He had to learn patience. He often felt nothing seemed to happen or move fast enough for him. Along with this vigor came a run-in with the law for speeding and how uncomfortable he was in check-out lines and similar situations. *I'll work at it*, he thought to himself. This zest was a step ahead of logic.

Change habits or hobbies and you'll change friends, he often thought. He walked into the bowling alley, and there was Ted. Ted, a good guy in his early sixties, devoted a good hunk of his life to this game. He liked to coach people. He gave me a few good pointers. His dream now was to spot a young one and, with his knowledge about the game, take him to championship ranks. "Ya, Ted, I've been doing chin-ups a couple times a week. My games been improving." The two had some small talk. Somewhat satisfied with his bowling that week, he was now off to the racetrack.

As he drove, he thought how the pleasant clear weather the past few days would have the track at ideal conditions as far as the handicappers' choices go. He could think of no good reason not to go along with them today. As he entered the grandstand area, the announcer called, "Twelve minutes, twelve minutes to post for the seventh race." As he walked farther, he saw John, racetrack John that is.

"You got anything goin'?" Chet asked.

"Meadow lass in the ninth," John said. "She can't lose!"

"So it's a day for favorites, huh, John?"

"Yeah, I've caught a bunch today. They're not payin' nothin' though."

"Why not?" Chad thought, *Start with a 1,500 bet for a triple parlay.*

"Can I get you for a ride to thirteenth when this is all over?"

"Sure," Chet said.

"Meet you over by the east snack bar."

So the two melted in with the crowd of horse players and, as usual, rarely felt a dull moment. The parlay came through, but it was not anything to write home about. Chad dropped off John as he said he would.

It was 5:45, and Chad felt like he could use a little nap. He drove home, lay down on the couch, and was out like a light in a matter of minutes.

An hour and a half later, Chad awakened and ate some tofu and rye bread then something sweet. On Saturday night, he thought, *I'll go over to the variety club later and see if I can get a dance.*

He wiped off his well-shined shoes that he wore when he was steppin' out.

It didn't take very long for a waiting female to look his way. Chad walked over to the attractive lady in a long black dress. "Would you like to dance?" Chet asked. She eagerly said sure with a wanting smile. The "Twist" song was playing as both shortly a roused each other's sex interests, then danced another, and softly parted company.

Not caring for alcohol in situations like this, Chad sipped at his cola drink. He saw a young lady that appeared to be alone, and so he walked over and introduced himself—a little small talk that didn't last too long—and Chad soon walked out the door. He enjoyed the music and dancing of these places and took them for that.

It's Sunday and dinner at Mom's. "Hi, Ma." Chad heads for the kitchen, lifts the lid of the roasting pan where lies a brown roast beef. His mother was making the gravy. "It'll be ready in just a little while. Oh, why don't you check the dryer?" Chad walks into the laundry room, turns a few switches, and discovers it's just a blown fuse. This symbiotic mother-son relationship worked out well. Chad doesn't really have time to cook himself healthy home-style meals or a wife. Mom isn't very handy around the condo. Dad passed away several years ago.

"It's time for my pills," Mom says as Chad fills his plate with food. Later, his mother would fill some plastic containers with the same food stuff that Chad would reheat later that week. After his meal, Chad relaxed on the couch for a good half hour. "I'll be on my way. Ma, is there anything else I can do before I go?" "No," his mother said. She walked with him to the door. He kissed her cheek and gave her a hug.

Well, it's Monday. Chad was shaving. He thought to himself that he didn't use to feel this spirited on Mondays. It must be because he has a dream now. After talking to Matt, he knew now his plans for Baani were at reality's doorstep. Ah, don't question it too much.

Chad arrives at work at ten minutes to four. As usual, Mohammed, the dock foreman, doesn't say hello. Only a side glance to acknowledge my presence. Mohammed, so to speak, is also the main security person. I guess he is suspicious of everyone because cigarettes or alcohol, the products Baani makes, can be easily sold if stolen.

Mohammed is the person that tells when I'm to go and pick up the fragrance oils. I'll do my best not to show any changes in my behavior. Anything like that may cause him to change my job.

One of my duties at the plant was to check employee bags as they left the building. A few years' experience in security told me when someone was stealing. Unless they were really going too far with the amount they were taking or if I had a notice from the office, I would just let it go. It wasn't worth it for anyone involved. I guess some had a touch of kleptomania. They may have wanted a few extra bucks or they were escaping boredom.

There was still some fine-tuning I had to do on the plans for Baani. I also had to know where I was going after the goods were sold. I would have to keep a low profile for about two years. The first place that came to mind was Sierra Vista, Arizona, a small town just outside the fort I was stationed at during some military training. Something else I had to do was to figure out how to tell my Kin that I was okay and not to fret.

A few months passed and Chad had created much optimism that his plan would be a success. So much so that he felt as though he had inherited a great deal of money and was just waiting for the red tape details to go through.

It wasn't much longer and one approached me with an envelope with plane tickets and said September 15. A good part of the reason I brought the oil back is that sending it over here without an escort made it untouchable as far as insurance was concerned.

So now was the time. A few days later, I called the number in New Delhi. The buyer would meet me at a roadside rest area about thirty miles outside of New Delhi. A complete exchange of vehicles would take place.

Now it's time to call Matt and get him primed. He would take a leave of absence. He hadn't decided yet whether he would continue working for the trucking firm or not and for how much longer anyway.

"Matt, you'll take a flight on September 28. You have the address of where you will pick up the van. You'll be staying at the Zaba Hotel, where you will wait patiently for a call from me when to meet me at the airport. There is a good chance the original containers have tracking devices on them. While you're driving, I'll be changing the oils into the drums that you will also bring. We will then dispose of the empty containers."

Chad always felt like a bit of an outsider as far as his family was concerned. Just the same when he thought too long about leaving his family and Chicago he would start to feel sentimental. His brother Joe had planned a surprise party for his mother's seventieth birthday. This would give him a chance to see them all before his September 15 trip. It would be quite some time before it would be safe for him to make any contact other than letting them know he was okay. He had been away before and learned the price of adventure includes intermittent loneliness.

It was like *boom!* the night before he was to leave and just before he was to pop a beer. Chad went over a checklist, and all figured to go well. So he drank the usual two beers and ate a little cheese. He also used a relaxation technique and hoped to get a good sleep.

He awoke at 11:00 a.m. His flight was to leave at 4:00 p.m. A small piece of tofu with a sweet roll sounded good. He looked at the bag, thinking he had placed the pair of earrings in it, a gift for Ida, the girl who helped him along while in the plantation. Looking out the window, the cab pulled up. It would be an hour before he'd set foot in the terminal. Ironic but not unusual, the driver looked very much to be Indian. "It's $27," the driver said. I was going to ask for a five back from the two twenties but then thought to give this guy a good day.

The flight attendant showed him his seat next to the window. It was an overcast day in Chicago. Conditions would change many times, mostly below him by the time he reached New Delhi. A few minutes later, a man who looked to be in his early twenties sat next to him in the aisle seat.

Both seemed to have looks of joy on their faces when the No Smoking sign went off and they both lit up. "A beer for me," said the young man to the attendant.

Except for refueling, it was a nonstop flight, and the young man thought he'd introduce himself. "My name is Mark, Mark James" as the two reached out their hands.

"Chad Kraine," I said. "What is taking you to exotic India?"

Mark said he was a fourth-year zoology major who won a grant for this trip to study Indian elephants.

"I'm on a business trip for my company," I told him.

A James Bond movie won the vote for what we'd watch during our flight. We were given a selection of four, and it certainly was my choice. So the two of us sat there and ate our fried chicken, neither to be having a care in the world.

The movie ended. I opened the shade to a star-filled sky, and why not? I made a wish. I let my seat recline, and at the blink of an eye, a female attendant was handing me a pillow. Before I dozed off, I lay with my eyes closed and had thoughts of Ida, the girl from the plantation and the Shangri-la week I had with her on my last visit. I didn't know very well that thinking of her gave me much happiness. I could see her face, her large brown eyes smiling contagiously with joy.

About an hour and a half later, I awoke and stretched my arms the best I could. "Did you enjoy your nap, sir?" Mary, the attendant, asked me with a slight accent that said she was from New York or maybe close enough.

"Why, yes, thank you, Mary," I said. "Could you bring me some coffee?"

"Yes," she said. Mark heard that and was also coming out of the slumber zone.

"Me too," he said.

Time seemed to be passing quickly, much faster than I expected. Before I knew it, the pilot announced we would begin our descent from thirty thousand feet. This was always something of a nature show this time of year. The layers and layers of cloud we passed through, all of them unique.

The descent usually lasts about two hours. And I grabbed a magazine for a touch of more stimuli.

We landed unto a wet steaming pavement. The rain had stopped, and I was glad. I wasn't really up to catching the charter plane to the plantation today. I grabbed a cab to the local airport hotel where I'd have a meal, shower, and a bed. I thought I'd play a little blackjack after a long-awaited horizontal nap.

The following day, my luck was better. There was a Learjet available to fly me to the plantation. When we landed, the rugged-looking four-wheel drive was there to pick me up. "Hello, Sahib." The familiar-looking driver walked over and reached for my suitcase. Welcome, he said. Thanks, I said. I got on board for the short ride to the cottage where I'd be staying for one to two weeks.

"Wednesday will be harvest party," the driver said. A festival of sorts was given about every four months in honor of the flower crop. We pulled up in front of the small white cottage with various wooden art pieces on the grass of the front yard, which included a spinning wheel. As I opened the door, there was a middle-aged woman wiping the kitchen area. Just finishing she said. I got myself a glass of sit-down water and let my mind go blank for a few seconds.

A light snack seemed to be in order. The place was moderately stocked. I sat down to some nuts, cheese, and an apple. There was a knock at the door. "It's open," I said.

"Hi, Chad," Ida said.

I said, "You're looking good."

"We've got to top you off with a little sun, yes, to cover up that bald spot."

"Bald spot!" I shouted. "What bald spot?" I jumped from my chair toward the mirror.

She laughed, "Just kidding, ha ha."

"I brought you a few things." She blushed. "I guess I could have waited for a better time."

"How was your trip over here?" she asked.

"Okay," I said. "Yes, my timing of gift of me because one of the items wasn't exactly afternoon wear."

There were many things I liked about this sweet lady. She had a little too much of a subordinate personality when I first met her. That has changed. Some of me must have rubbed off on her. I don't think I want it to manifest any further though.

"Thank you," she said. "Thanks." She touched my hand gently and kissed my cheek.

"How about a little something to drink?" I asked her.

"Yes, okay."

"Can of pop?"

"Hmm, yeah!"

We sit there while I finished my snack. She nibbled a few pieces also. Summer was ending back in the States. I guess I never was much for getting a suntan. We walked down a path that was heavily shaded by a canopy of overhanging tree limbs, and the moderate breeze coming through couldn't have felt better.

"How are your girlfriends in Chicago?" she asked in somewhat angry and jealous tone.

"Which one do you want to hear about? Ha ha," I said and drew away from her as she motioned she was going to slap my arm.

"Oh you," she cried.

We walked for about twenty minutes; I was ready for a shower. Afterward, we ate, played a few games of cards, then watched some TV. She then returned to her place

The following day, I had a little work to do. One of my other duties was to test the fragrance oil for quality compared to the prior shipment. I used a light meter. A beam of light passed through a glass container, which resembled a store-bought ant farm. The light then registered on an absorbing slate, which then gave a reading whether or not this load had the same or close to the same molecular structure as the previously purchased oil. That was about all I knew or all I really had to know about it.

I came outside and started the Volkswagen. An auto of some kind was always loaned to me during my stays. I drove to the building where the finished products were stored, one of many.

I recalled my first trip over here and the tour I was given of the plantation.

To my right was building, where the flowers are initially processed. It was the largest building but a mere speck of the forty thousand acres of which it was part of. The building was pretty much exactly the same as it has been for the last three centuries. Most of the building were occupied by small wooden extraction presses, which were operated manually. This method was used because it was thought that any other means would contaminate the product.

There were some 3,500 people working on the plantation. A number of the families can be dated back with the Shinow clan. They started the whole thing and still maintain the largest percentage of shares and control since the early 1700s.

The oil test was satisfactory, and I thought I'd drive to a nearby town and do a little shopping. The drive was scenic. There was a Buddhist monastery, and pagodas dotted the green vegetation.

When I returned to the cottage, Lena, the other house lady, was preparing my supper—fried shrimp with rice and sauce. I was starving, and the aroma doubled my appetite. "This is delicious," I said to Lena. "The sauce is like something I never tasted before."

I finished my supper and thought I'd walk over by Mike's. He was a handyman, landscaper, etc., in this area. I knocked on his door. "Chad," he said as he opened the screen door. "Oh, you're here for some more chess lessons."

"Yeah, I guess I am, ha ha." He walked over and got me a beer along with a glass.

"Relax," he said. "I'll have things set up in just a minute." As he did, I figured to give him a good dame since it would be our last.

"Hey, I'm getting married," he said. "Yeah, I know, I'm crazy! You'll crack up one of these days yourself, Chet."

"Yeah," I said as I gave out a laugh.

This wasn't a bad way to spend an evening. As I walked back to the cottage, I realized my education had been furthered.

So I had one more beer, and then I hit the sack. I should be getting used to this bed by now. When I awoke the next day, there was no house lady, so I cooked myself a couple of eggs. They must be busy elsewhere, getting ready for the festival. I drank an extra cup of coffee and made a mental rehearsal of the way I wanted my plan to work out. Bluntly, Matt was going to meet me with the van, then we would drive over to meet the buyer, keeping cool and thinking clearly.

"Ida!" She startled me as if I had been talking out loud. I guess this would be as good as time as ever to let her know where she fits into the picture, providing she wanted to. "It all sounds so, so big, Chad. I'd like to think it over. Going to the States and living with someone hot?" she said with a questioning tone. "I have my family here, and I have to consider them also."

"OK," I said, "think it over then. I don't want you to get involved unless you think you'll be happy. I'll write to you. I will be using the alias James Bicot when I do."

"Let's go over and help get things ready for the festival tonight." So we did. Somehow, I got the job of peeling onions. I didn't cry while doing it though. It was two o'clock when I came back to the cottage. I felt like a nap would ensure a fun time tonight.

I awoke an hour and a half later to the sound of a chattering mongoose. I hoped it was because he was hungry and not because he had seen the unwanted. This was open country, and I was glad he was up and about.

I was to pick up Ida at five o'clock. I guess a piece of fruit should hold me over until I start eating there. Ida said all I think about is food. I figured she was about 80 percent right.

It was a pretty warm day, and when I drove up, she was wearing an apropos bikini-type top. "You look fantastic," I said. She stroked back her hair and said thanks.

The event was set on a slight ascent. As we approached, there must have been thirty or more open-sided brightly striped tents that said welcome. I was very hungry and thought it best to restrain myself a little. After all, this party was going to be here for three days. That's all Ida said as I placed two thin slices of pork on my plate. I've got time, I said.

The band was setting up. They looked to be from South America or something like that. We sat down with some others while we ate.

Atas Shinow gave a little speech, thanking all for their work, for the good crop, and nature's important role. In closing, he said to enjoy yourselves.

There were acrobats and a tiger act. These ended as the sun was setting.

Then the band took over. We danced a fast one—a mixture of the twist and what I thought the music was telling me to do.

Neither one of us got mushy during the waltz. During one of the band breaks, a comedian came on. I had a bit more to eat and then called it an evening.

The day before I was to leave, I slept until twelve. Ida came over. We let it be understood that we were not totally committed to each other, possibly later. For now, we were both free to do as we pleased.

We went for a swim that afternoon. I couldn't come out of the water. I stood there and drew in a deep breath. She looked at me like no woman ever did before. I felt strong.

At the cottage, we ate supper. Tomorrow was going to be a busy day for me. Today would be made as enjoyable as possible for it would be quite sometime we'd be together again.

I said, "I thought it best if we made our separation today. I didn't want to risk my getting too emotional when I had so much to do and think about the next day."

"Take care," she said. "Write as soon as you can." My eyes were the first to get glassy.

Yes, emotional I became, but just the same, I didn't really have any trouble falling asleep that night. I awoke the next morning at ten thirty. Take off time was 1:00 p.m. My optimism on the way things would go became speckled with a bit of nervousness, and I don't give a damn since there were so many factors I had no control over.

The small truck arrived on time with the cargo. Why shouldn't the rest of the steps be the same way? The driver and I loaded the two drums into the plane with the pilot telling us where the best place for balance would be. This was the smallest aircraft I've been on in all my trips. It was a new experience. Talk about being in the air.

When we landed in New Delhi, I called Matt at the hotel. "Hello, Matt. I'm at gate number eight. If you have any trouble, call 84311, the number I'm calling from." While I waited for him, I bought a coffee from the vending machine and ate the peanut butter sandwich I made before I left. Matt arrived in the van a half hour later. We quickly loaded the drums. Now time to call the man with the money.

I felt my heart begin to race as I listened to his phone ring the fourth time. Five, bingo! He picked up. "Hello," the familiar voice at the other end said.

"Yes, hello, this is Chad."

"Okay, Chad, we'll see you there at six o'clock."

"We're all set, Matt," he said. "Six o'clock, let's go. We should get there a little early."

Chad changed the fragrance oil into the different drums while Matt drove down the highway.

When we arrived at the rest area, the buyer was already there. I somehow wanted more to take place for the amount of money we were going to make. That was it though. We exchanged vehicles and drove off. A little way down the highway, I let out a laugh, then Matt also laughed and put some music on!

Now at the hotel, Matt said our plane leaves at 1:00 p.m. tomorrow as he just spoke with reservations.

That night, both guys, filled with elation and nervousness, in no way could lie down and go to sleep. They decide what would do them a world of good is a nice mile or so walk. When they return, they downed some beers and smoked cigarettes. They talked about when they were in their early teens. "Yeah, remember when we used to camp out of the park? Yeah, we're still kinda crazy!" Shortly, Matt was asleep.

Chad's thought was, *I'm not going to squander this money. Well, maybe 25 percent or so.* He made a list of the things he wanted to do. Let's start real slow. Bird watching, horseback riding, an Alaskan photography trip, snow skiing, a trip to Paris via an Atlantic cruise ship during the crisp autumn months. Something he wanted to do very much now was to get married and raise some kids. *Right after I burn off most of this energy.* He thought about those last two for a minute and laughed a little.

A lot of changes were going to take place in Chad's life. He had been working as security and held jobs as cab driver, all of which consisted of a lot of weekend work. In a big way, it had been self-chosen. Now he wanted to feel what it was like to be in the mainstream. But for now, gradually he wound down and fell asleep.

I'm going to put this fake beard and sunglasses on. Landing time in LA was still in question. We'll get there though.

Chad went on to that small town, Sierra Vista, Arizona, which was right outside the fort he was stationed at while in the military some twenty-five years ago. Matt went back to Chicago. He wanted to be close to his kids I guess.

One of the benefiting factors about Sierra Vista was its elevation—five thousand feet above sea level. Even when it got to be 90 percent or so, it was dry heat and still very comfortable. When it's 100 percent in Phoenix, it's 80 percent here, almost always a 20 percent difference.

There were a lot of things I had to do, but for now, I'm just going to check into this motel.

Chet awoke at 1:30 p.m. to noise coming from the bathroom. "Who's in here?" he asked with a very asking tone in his voice. "Maid service," came the answer. "I go home at two o'clock." Chad now recalling asking her to come back later when she knocked about 10:00 a.m., looking toward the bathroom. He quickly hopped out of bed and put on his trousers. Soon the maid stepped out.

Chad stroked the side of his head, saying "I've been working kind of hard the past couple of weeks. It really feels good to get some extra rest." The maid was thinking, *I know what else would make this boy feel good!* The black medium-sized woman with equally colored nylon hose that covered heart-throbbing ankles stood by the bathroom door. Her loose-fit organizational dress revealed a shining bra as she raised her arm. The body language she was giving gave him no reason to be shy or embarrassed about the erection bulging in his pants.

She walked over to him in a submissive manner and, for a second, cast her eyes down. She stroked his arm while asking him, "How long you gonna be staying?" He then put his arm around the waist that was lifted toward him, then their eager mouths met. She ended the kiss in about five seconds and then turned her back to him.

He nuzzled her neck as she raised her dress. She then slipped down her panties and hose a few inches below her buttocks. It was wet, hard, and fast!

After that, I took a shower and, for a second, was confused about what time of day it was. I had a light snack with some decaf and then smoked a cigarette. Things were really hitting the spot.

A thirty-minute nap seemed to be in order. I set the alarm.

Now it's out time. He dresses up and puts a good shine on his shoes. First, it's out to supper at 6:30 p.m. at the nearby restaurant—some eggs, a small steak, American fried potatoes, coffee, and toast with a touch of jelly. I sat there content, optimistic, without a care in the world. "Waitress, would you bring me the paper please?" So I started with the funnies, then the front page, and finally the lineup at the dog track.

It was an hour's drive to Tucson where the track was located. Why not? I was in the mood for a ride. The auto rental was a stone's throw away, and I was off. While at the track, he has a beer or two and light conversation with a dog handler who gave him a few winners.

He returns to the motel, has a light snack, and then to sleep.

With all the new things going on in my life, my routine exercise workouts were somewhat neglected. Now that I was going to be in one place for a while, maintaining them would be easier. Calisthenics, then jogging the next day, swimming or the gym bar on the third day. It took quite a bit of time from my life, but I wouldn't give it up for the world. The benefits were well worth it.

Today, I had to go find myself an apartment. I headed over to what appeared to be a newly built apartment complex. I rang the bell at the manager's office. A woman with sandy brown hair gave me a quick look over through the door window while unlocking it.

"Yes, can I help you?" she asked.

"Yes, what I had in mind was a quiet one-bedroom apartment with a northern exposure."

"I think we'll be able to accommodate you. Let's start with the model." So we walked over about a hundred feet. After mulling around a bit, I asked about the price.

"It's 340 a month," she said. "One-year lease with one month's security deposit."

"Fine, I'll take it," I said. We did the paperwork; I gave her the cash.

"My name is Pat," she said as she handed me a business card. "If you have any questions, you can come to the office or call either of the two numbers on the card."

Something told me I was going to like it here. Most people here are newcomers to the area like myself, a social situation I will feel comfortable at.

Included in the complex were a swimming pool, tennis court, and game room. There was more than enough to do.

I spent the remainder of the day buying a bedroom set and television. Enough business for the day, I went back to the motel and had a pizza delivered. I thought about the different areas of my life while I watched TV. Later, two beers set me right for a good night's sleep.

I awoke the next morning excited. Who wouldn't be? I'm going to Tucson today to look around for a new car, nothing crazy like my first impulse, more like a Buick—midsize, sporty with most of the extras. I packed an overnight bag. Rushing is not the thing to do when buying a car.

I walked over to the black car with a thin white stripe on the side. It had leather seats with a good music system. The salesman asked, "So you think this is you?"

"For the most part, yeah," I said. That didn't take very long. I felt like things were moving along faster than they should. So I checked into a motel to bring myself down a little. I bought some root beer and pretzels and figured I'd watch some soap operas. I then snoozed on the reclining chair for a while.

Later, I went to a restaurant and had a wholesome meal of roast beef with mashed potatoes and read the paper. I then took a short stroll and sat in the park and let my meal digest.

There were people playing shuffle board as the sun was low.

Then to one of my favorite pastimes. *I'll bowl a couple of games,* I thought. Not bad. A 177+190 with a house ball. As I was paying for the games, I saw a poster that read Mac's Beer $70,000 Open Bowling Tournament, to be held the day after tomorrow. Just then, I felt a surge of energy come to me. What else could I do? "Young lady, would you please give me an entry form for the tournament?"

I guess I was about due for a new bowling ball and shoes anyway. I went over to the small shop. In the establishment and stuck with the same kind of ball I had been using, the AKER sledge. I called Pat to please watch for and let the furniture delivery men in.

Check-in time for the tournament was 4:00 p.m. After I carried my ball a block and a half, I was at the door at 3:45 p.m. I'm a light smoker myself but was still glad the event was going to be no smoking. The guy at the counter gave me my card. My number was 57. I was to bowl on lanes nine and ten and scheduled to bowl six games, six different opponents. That is, you continue to bowl providing you keep winning. I won the first three games easily; however, I had to talk myself down a little on the third games as I started to feel more tension than was beneficial.

A forty-minute break followed the first three games. I walked over to what could be called an extended dining area. I spotted a seat! "Anyone sitting here?" I openly asked those sitting at the raised table. No one replied, so I sat down to my one-half peanut butter and jelly sandwich. "Are you still in?" the guy in the brown-and-white checkered board shirt asked. I said yeah in a humble voice. "We're out of this one. There's one next month in flagstaff," he said. I did my best at resting up and tried to keep conversation to a minimum and still trying to let them know I was a bowling buddy. I then took a light stroll to the men's room.

And you said you were going to lie low for a while!

When I returned, the porter had just finished giving the lanes a light coat of oil. They work very well for me that way. I always had a little difficulty in competition with women. My fifth game was scheduled with a Harriet Bock. This was the '90s, and I told myself to just play your own game.

On my sixth game, I was on my eighth frame with a clean game going. As I drew back to pick up a spare, I heard a loud bang. I missed my shot. I thought for a second it was deliberate on the part of someone that didn't want me to win. I composed myself and thought this is all part of it. Something you have to put up with. By the skin of my teeth, I won the game.

I was exhausted! I need a good meal first of all—two pork chops, mashed potatoes, and green beans. "Waitress, I'll have a piece of that cherry pie." My system was in full swing. I then relaxed with the newspaper, looking for some of the lighter things happening in the area. I watched some television at the motel, then went for a short walk. I had the urge to call someone and share in my excitement as things were that was impossible. I decided to make some notes. I'd be able to tell them all about it later someday.

I was on my second drink and started to nod off in the chair. With some of the tension I'd be feeling tomorrow, this sense of heaviness is just what I needed.

I awoke at twelve noon and had some toast and tea. I would want to eat a larger meal at two o'clock; check-in time was at 4:00 p.m. I listened to the radio. They were talking about TV game shows.

The setup was different today. I was to bowl two games with an opponent. The total of the two games would be added. The one with the higher score would then bowl another opponent. The higher score of this match would then stand and be played against all others. From the two game totals, the higher score would then be first place.

The crowd at the bowling alley was smaller today, but much more serious. In my first game, it was the sixth frame, and I was working on my fifth straight strike. I was truly at my best. I had hypnotized myself. All my physical and mental energies were going through a magnifying glass with the hot spot right on this bowling tournament. The second pair of games gave me a score of 487 to defeat a man named Bob Hentel. There were still persons bowling, but my score was now on top.

I felt my self-discipline had given me an edge. My thoughts were that I deserved to win. I had to admit I was anxious; I was standing about ten yards from the officials watching the second from the last pair of bowler's hand in their score sheet. A few minutes and some nervous pacing later, I walked up the last two bowlers. They gave their score sheet to the well-dressed gray-haired man who was almost as restless as myself. He looked at the scores and then gave me a slight grin. He then reached for the microphone. "Ladies and gentleman, we have a high score of 487 belonging to Chad Holtas."

"Come on up here, Chad!" So I walked onto the slightly raised stage. The representative of Mac's Beer and the owner of the bowling alley, their faces with joyous expressions, greeted me. "Chad, are you surprised?" asked the beer rep. Then he answered his own question, "No, not at all. Are you?

"Well, a little," I said with a slight laugh.

"Congratulations, Chad," the owner said as he lay his hand on my shoulder and reached for my hand.

"May we have the trophy please. Chad, on behalf of Mac's Beer and Cactus Lanes, I'd like to present you with this trophy." There was an applause.

"Thank you," I said. "Thank you."

"And also, Chad, we have this check for $40,000." Another applause sang through the atmosphere. Once again, I said a sincere thank you. So the pinnacle of the day had been reached. I took a deep breath and started to feel a bit more relaxed. The spotlight was dimming.

"Chad, how about having dinner with us tomorrow evening?"

"Hmm, yeah, yeah, sure," I said.

"Okay fine, we'll be at the Halcyon over Albon St., seven o'clock."

"Sounds good," I said.

"Chad, tell the hostess you're with the Bill Grant party." He was the owner of the bowling alley.

The next day, Chad stood in front of the mirror, combing his dark brown hair. He strained his eyes to make sure the few grays were still there. His mustache, he thought, matched perfectly. As I approached the restaurant, I saw a valet for the cars, something new for me. The place looked dark and fancy. I felt my stomach to be a little jittery.

"Can I help you, sir?"

"Yes, I'm with the Bill Grant party." The hostess brought me over to the semi-closed-off dining area.

I drew in a half deep breath and glanced for Bill. "Chad," Bill said in a friendly tone.

"Everyone! To those of you who don't know, Chad here is the winner of our tournament." The hostess sat me down next to an attractive lady. "Chad, that's my sister Lisa. Lisa, meet Chad."

"Hi, Lisa," I said. The servers were just then laying out the food—roast beef sliced with pride, fried chicken, mashed potatoes, and gravy. It dissipated the tension. I was there mainly to eat. The table of about twenty saw things in pretty much the same way; we dug in. As we satisfied our hunger, people began to talk more. The couple across from me spoke of their two to twelve flat apartment buildings. Then I guess they wanted to know what else I did besides bowl.

"I'm marketing a few items, yes, martial arts training equipment."

"That's interesting, Chad. My name is Fred," one of the guys across the table said. "My employment standing didn't go much further than that, and I couldn't have been happier." I talked a little with Lisa. She said she was involved with volunteer work with Apache Indians in the area. She wasted no time recruiting someone she thought might have a couple of hours a week to spare. As we exchanged phone numbers, I told her I would call her first chance I had. So the evening simmered down. "Keep in touch," Bill said as I was getting ready to leave. "Nice meeting you, Chad" also rang out a few times.

As I sat down in my motel room, it was now just soaking in that I had won the tournament. I had never won anything near this dimension, and it felt good.

The next day, I awoke and thought it best to get busy again. Now where was I? If I remember right, I had just bought that new car out there and had furniture delivered to my apartment. I checked out of the motel and returned to Sierra Vista.

I had this need to communicate with someone I knew for a while. I wrote a letter to Ida using the alias. I let her know all went well and that all is well now. I only told her partly on what was going on now, thinking her life might not be quite as exciting. I did not ask whether she had made a decision about joining me. That would come in time. I closed the letter, thinking of you.

I bought a few extras for the apartment, a painting of people having a picnic, some knickknacks, and an aquarium with five pairs of guppies and two pairs of black mollies.

I was working on a few ideas in the martial arts, but that I considered to be in the same category as the fish, kind of a hobby. I looked at the clock, five fifteen. Time was going by so quickly. I could scarcely believe it. Then the guy said, "My name is Ben. I live next door here. Can I talk to you a minute?"

"Sure," I said, "come on in."

"I'm not sure if my air conditioner is running right. It's on about forty-five minutes out of every hour. How's yours working?" he asked. "Well, as far as today is concerned, just the opposite of yours. It runs about fifteen minutes out of every hour. That keeps it at about 75 percent in here. Well yeah, that's what I thought 'cause it really hasn't been that hot. I'm going to call them to have the maintenance guy check it out. You said your name is Ben. Mine's Chad." We shook hands. "Would you care for a beer? Sounds good? Strange that the air conditioner would be acting up building being new and all. Things happen like that sometimes."

Ben said he did oil paintings and photography, mostly portraits, but anything that helped pay the rent. He was about my age and agreed we play a game of racket ball someday.

I sat down to a glass of iced tea. I thought about investing some of this money. I got out the phone book to find it broken. What luck. There's one right in the same building where I do my banking. "The next afternoon," I said.

"What time?" Bill asked.

"About two," I answered.

"Super," he said. "I'll see you then."

It was about a ten-minute drive down there from my apartment. On the way, I said to myself I was going to be rigid in what I wanted to invest in. I wasn't about to let this guy talk me into moon mining or anything like that. I had given this matter quite a bit of thought and felt the recreation area was going to progress upward, and Munwick Corporation was where my money was going to be.

As I stood before the sliding glass window, a very attractive woman opened it. "Yes, my name is Chad. I'm here to see Bill Riley." She stood up and gave me the second punch. She opened the door and showed me to Bill's office. The preliminaries were short. Bill got to the point. "How much money are we talking about here, Chad?"

"I figure about $40,000 total."

"I've got a few hot ones I could steer you onto." When he said the word *hot*, for a few seconds, that's just what I felt. "Munwick sounds good, Chad." We did a little more paperwork, shook hands, and I was on my way!

This never a dull moment. Lifestyle was having an aphrodisiac effect on me. I wanted some female companionship. I had Lisa's number. It was going to cost me to go out with her. Right, that volunteer work. "Hello.

"Hello, Lisa, this is Chad. How are you doing?"

"Fine," she said in a very pleasant voice. "And you?" she asked.

"I'm doin' all right," I said.

"I was wondering if you like to have dinner and see a show or something."

"Sounds good to me," she said.

"Is there something you'd like to see?" I asked.

"Yes, as a matter of fact, there's a plan called Where's Harry? It's comedy, and I heard it's hilarious. Let me get the tickets."

"Really?" I asked.

"I'll call you back with the day and time," she said. So she called me the following day. Tickets were for the day after at eight. I went over there at seven fifteen. *Bzzz!* "Come on up," she said over the intercom.

"Oh, a rose for me? How nice."

"You look great."

"Thanks, I'll be about five minutes yet."

"You tell me how to get there. I got kind of medium seats, is that okay with you?"

"Fine," I said. "I'll have the lasagna, okay?"

Two lasagnas it'll be over our apple slices. "Chad, can you spare a half day once a week?"

"Mmm, yeah!"

"Good, we need someone to give an educational program on the prevention of alcohol abuse. It will involve a half-hour video, some literature, and perhaps a short talk by you, Chad. This will be to kids between the ages of nine and fourteen."

"That doesn't sound too complicated," I said.

"I'll go with you on your first trip."

"Well, that'll make it even better," I said.

After the show, I went over to her place for drinks and some soft music. I wound up leaving about 2:00 a.m.

Six months had passed since coming to Arizona and my time was occupied by many things, but very seldom boredom.

I was enjoying myself gong to the different schools, educating these young people about alcohol abuse. I was taking good care of myself, eating well, exercising, and getting plenty of rest.

I wrote to Ida three times and was yet to receive a letter from her. It's true we had no real commitment to each other, but I really wanted to hear from her anyway. I began to think she was seriously involved with someone else. Two weeks ago, I mailed a letter bluntly begging her to write to me.

Some time passed, and I finally got a piece of mail. It was the last letter I wrote her. It had been unopened, stating no such person that is the alias she was to use lived at that address. This really put a bunch of questions in my mind.

She had an older sister. I wrote to her, stating I was a female friend that Ida attended college with some years back.

I then felt like a little vacation. I decided to go marlin fishing off the coast of Mexico. I walked into the local travel office. The lady there was quick to send me off in just two days. I planned a one-week stay at the busiest tourist center at this time of year.

When the plane landed, it began to storm rather heavily. That was pretty much the picture for my seven-day stay. Although I didn't have the excitement of a large fish on my line, the storms, along with weather warning, did not allow my heartbeat to fall below the normal rate. I hit a couple of discos and enjoyed some exotic seafood; all in all, I had a good time. The hotel manager's closing remarks, "Come again someday, señor."

When I returned to Arizona, it felt home more than ever. A few weeks went by. Aha, response from the letter I wrote to Ida's sister.

The letter read as follows:

> Dear Rebecka,
>   We were very happy that a friend would
> inquire about Ida. However, I wish it were better

news that I had to tell you. My sister Ida passed away four months ago. She suffered a fatal snakebite. All efforts were made to save her, such as serums, but were not in time as she was alone when the incident occurred. She was found unconscious, and it was quite some time before we knew what was wrong. On behalf of myself and family, we wish you well.

Sincerely,
Mara

I was saddened very much by this letter. I did care for Ida a great deal. My emotions made me aware she was a big part of my life. I did not cry often, but this was a time I didn't hold back on what I was feeling.

Many times, when I thought of the future, she was in the picture.

Now she was no longer on this earth.

I felt frantic. My hands trembled. I needed to pull myself together. I mixed myself a drink, sat down, and did my best to relax my mind and body.

I thought it best I should talk to someone even if it were only for today. I suspected this first day would be the hardest. I looked in the phone book and asked if I could make an appointment to talk to a clergy at one of the rectory that night and talked to father Norman. He advised me to do some things that, at the time, I didn't really think of because of my grief, such as keeping myself busy. It's normal to grieve someone who has passed away, but you can't let it stop you. I said, "Thank you, Father." "Chad, here's a church bulletin, feel free to come by again."

As I drove home, I remembered him saying this too shall pass. I prayed for her. I had a picture of her in my wallet.

Two years passed by since camping to Arizona, and I can truly say I like it here. I work part-time at a small ceramics shop and also do some sculpting at home. I'm still working with the kid's alcohol abuse prevention program and maintaining a friendship with Lisa and dating her.

I thought it was about time I took that ocean cruise. It was late October. I called the travel agent. He said he could set me up to leave November 3. I wanted to cross the Atlantic during this chilly crisp time of year. A tropical cruise would come something later.

On November 6, I was standing on the ship's deck with a steaming cup of coffee, looking out at the horizon with a Danish to boot, then I smoked a cigarette. To remember one of my favorite performers, how sweet it is.

I took a walk downstairs to what they called the game room. Women were, of course, allowed in much was organized by the staff. There were card games. There was a guy in his sixties waiting to take someone on, so I played a game of checkers with him. "What kind of work do you do?" he asked. "I guess you could call me an entrepreneur," I said.

"I practiced law for thirty-three years, mostly in the St. Paul area. Transportation is what I specialized in representing trucking firms." Frank was his name. "I'm about due for something to eat," he said. My thoughts exactly. We went over to the twenty-four-hour snack bar.

"You do much dancing," he asked. "No," I said "not a real lot." "At three thirty, I'm going over for some lessons on ballroom dancing. It's all free of charge. Kind of comes along with the trip, I guess. Why don't you come along?" "Yeah, sure, why not?" I said.

Things went along very well, much easier than I thought and what didn't for right I called improvisation. After an hour and a half of this, I could certainly omit my calisthenic workout for today. Cora, my instructor, said there'll be a hot time on the old boat day after tomorrow. I said I'd be there.

The next day, I was excited about this dance business. I figured I'd go over and buy myself some new clothes. I had the sales guy help me pick out a few things that would keep me from clashing.

Ah, dance day. I was still feeling up there. The steps I learned should give me the confidence to enjoy myself. I got to the dance hall a little past the scheduled starting time. I first went to the bar to wet my whistle. I sipped at my drink and melted into the atmosphere of lights, music, and all that was alive. There was a switch from live band to DJ and music machine that would go back and forth all night.

Cora spotted me, raised her head slightly, and gave me a glad-to-see-you smile. She started to walk in my direction. "Hi Chad, how, you doin' tonight?"

"Revved up!" I said.

"Good," she said.

"Chad, when the band starts up again, I'll ask them to play something that's familiar to you."

"Terrific," I said.

"I'll talk to you later," she said.

There were some ladies who looked as though they came here to dance. So I went over and asked one of them. We moved to the sounds of the music machine. My body temperature was on the rise. We danced another, thanked each other, and separated. I sat around and gazed at the people, sometimes fixing my eyes a little longer than was polite. Just the same, it felt great to be here. I guess I had recovered from the previous dance and was ready to do it again.

My timing was in step with the rest of the dance. The band was back and, as Cora asked, started to play something familiar to me. It was an instrumental called "Leaf Flight." I looked around for someone to ask to dance when, to my right, a thin pretty lady tapped my shoulder. "Would you like to dance?" she asked. "Sure," I said with a startled tone. It was easy. There's nothing like practice before the event. "You're a good dancer," she said. "Thanks! I owe it all to my instructor. I did the same thing sometime back, took some lessons."

As we danced and spoke a little more, our breathing became apparent. We were tiring. "Well, I think that's enough for me," I said. "Yes, well, thank you," she said. We looked at each other as if we were both interested. I had to think fast. She helped me. "I'm thirsty," she said, "not for anything alcoholic though. I'm going to the ladies' room."

"I'll get one of these tables right over here," I said.

"Fine!" I ordered two pomegranates over ice.

"So tell me about yourself," I said.

"I'm divorced, no children. I, along with my brother and sister, operate a tooling company, which deals mostly with the auto industry." I then told her the basics about myself. Sharon was not on the shy side. A waltz began to play, and she asked, "Dance with me?" People in the dance hall slowly began to disappear. Sharon and I had been stimulated enough for the night and needed a rest so as not to let a good thing turn into overstress or whatever.

I helped her on with her beige shawl, actually just sort of touched it a little. "Thank you," she said with a smile. It was a beautiful night, a clear sky with a half moon and stars shined as we walked on deck. "I'm in section E," she said. A few steps more and we were at E door. I've entered everything seemed so quiet now. No one else was about. "Well, here we are, number 14. Thanks for everything," she said. "Give you a call," I said. "Sure," she said. She turned the key and the doorknob.

As I walked, I started to think where I was. I guess I was in a new relationship. I thought a beer would go good right about now. Yeah, on the enclosed deck area, just outside the bar and dance floor. "Let me have a bottle of beer," I said. I overheard a few people talking millions, as in two digits. One mentioned the name Sharon. If it is, it is! Then I walked over to the glassed deck. I liked the way things went that night and definitely was going to call her. I sat there a few more minutes, then headed for my cabin.

The following day, no plans were made. I just felt like getting myself together, my clothes, etc. A light calisthenics workout, some television, and make some plans for the next day. Tomorrow, I would call Sharon, maybe ask for a date. I also wanted to visit the casino. I heard they had nel. Games pick up.

I didn't really feel homesick or anything like that, but with the holidays coming up, via satellite, I thought it's a good time to call my family, brother.

"Yeah, Joe, it's Chad. Can you hear me? OK.

Synthetic or from a food source, your body doesn't know the difference and the benefits are the same. We had some sandwiches at a nearby table. Afterward, we all went our separate ways. Back at my cabin 43, I watched the last half of *Jeopardy* and decided I could use a nap.

Before I nodded out though, my phone rang. "Hello, Chad, this is Mike Parker, one of the assistant managers from the casino. Chad, you left your name here to let you know when there would be an organized poker game. Well, Chad we have a game set with five players for tonight at 8:00 p.m. Betting will range from one minimum to five maximum."

"Fine, thank you. I'll be there, bye now." Now for my nap.

At 6:00 p.m., I felt a little refreshed. I put on a light-colored shirt with dark pants and wiped off my shoes. I set my loss limit at $1,000. I wanted to enjoy myself and still keep things exciting and questioned whether the two could possibly be in gear at the same time. I figured I would drink beer and smoke like I usually did. Yeah, beer and cigarettes are especially satisfying when playing cards. Also, I thought about card games that turned out to be negative. The reasons too much pride or green, not thinking that is not keeping a cool head. Have fun. That should keep things in perspective.

After checking in at the desk, a guy brought me to a room, which had a double-sized opened doorway. I guess so we could still be in touch with the rest of the casino and vice versa. Three guys were already seated. None of them had serious looks on their faces. "How you doin' guys? My name's Chad." Then they introduced themselves as Phil, Don, and Ray.

The guy that brought me in had a name tag that I didn't notice until now. My head spun for a second or two. I just said to myself I would do my best at remembering names. Just then, the final of the five walked in. "Hello, gentlemen. I'm George."

And so we went into gambling. First game was straight poker. The manager called the waitress. "Check their drinks, Sara." I had the money. If you want good service and courtesy, you have to share your good fortune.

I remained in a good mood throughout the evening as I neared the finish of my fifth beer. It was a good time to estimate my winnings. I forgot my manners a bit and stretched back in my chair and yawned. It's never easy to give notice. You're ready to call it a night, especially when you're winning. At the start, we agreed to 12:30 a.m. as the quitting time and we were about twenty minutes away from it. I was up about seven hundred earlier times in my life. I would have been impressed, but relativity was in place. I gave a slight rise to my eyebrows.

"It was a pleasure playing cards with you, gentlemen. Maybe we can do it again sometime." Thy all gave me sort of a nod goodbye.

As I walked out of the casino, a stimuli of sort began to take me over. Ah, I think I'll go over to what could be called the ship's singles bar. Besides, I need a little more time for the game to settle. The bartender was giving a drink to a lady that seemed inviting I could enjoy some conversation. The bartender, Clair, and I then did share some small talk and smiles for about an hour. "You look like a nice guy," Clair said. The bartender went on somewhere. "Well, thanks," I said. "I try to be."

"Will you walk me to my room?" "Sure," I said. When we got there, she put her hand on my shoulder and gave me a light kiss. "Thanks," she said. As I walked away, I remembered her saying she had a female roommate. Nice night, I thought.

Early the next afternoon, Sharon called. "Hi, Chad, feeling your oats today? They're going to be playing volleyball on the outside court today about two o'clock." "Hmm, yeah sounds good." I was really beginning to believe we liked each other.

I felt safe they had the rubber padding down, ha ha ha. Somehow, Sharon and I were on different teams. I didn't like it for one reason. I kept watching her instead of keeping my mind on the game. The team I was on wound up winning anyway. "Sharon, I'm going to shower and stuff. How about you? And I'm having dinner later." "Okay. Fine," she said. "Knock on my door at seven."

The next two days, Sharon and I went swimming, did a little shopping and less sleeping. We were intimate but did not feel comfortable enough to have intercourse. We had seen a movie then thought it best if we separated for a while. It was sort of mental fatigue on both our part. That is, we were overstimulated the last few days and our burners needed to be turned down.

The course of sleep I had that night was restlessness followed by deep sleep, restlessness, and another deep sleep; however, I woke up rested. The can of shaving cream didn't seem to be giving out the foamy stuff it used to. So after eating, I figured I go over and buy some drugstore items.

On my way back, as I walked down the hallway, I had seen three guys standing in the area about where my room was. One of them was knocking. As I drew closer, yes, they were at my door. One of them had a familiar tome about him, but I couldn't place him.

"Yes, gentlemen, can I help you?"

"Are you Chad Bert?"

"Yes, I am," I said.

"We'd like to speak with you if we can."

"Sure, umm, step inside."

"Chad, my name is Tom Ascot," the man in uniform said. He was one of the ship's officers I guess. "Chad," he said, "first of all, you don't have to say anything or answer any questions any more than what you just did, that your name is Chad Bert. Chad, would you come down to the captain's office where we'll be able to tell you more about what is going on?"

"Okay. Yeah," I said. "Let me put these things down." I brushed my thighs, thinking whether or not I had all I would need. We were halfway there, yet not one of us uttered a word. Maybe I didn't want to admit it just yet. But I had a manifesting idea where I had seen the guy that seemed a little familiar.

The captain stood up as we entered his office. "Have a seat, gentleman." He sat back down and clasped his hands together. I was still feeling as cool as a cucumber.

"You're Chad Bert?" he asked.

"Yes, I am," I said.

"Chad, this man here, Abil Had, says he knew you when you called yourself Chad Pell. He says you're a strong suspect in the theft of over a million dollars' worth of fragrance oils or something of that nature. He also has given us a written and signed statement to that affect. At the moment, though, it best not to say anything until I spoke with a lawyer. Chad, we spoke with authorities in the United

States and France. Chad, when we reach port in France, police will be there to question you. It is my decision that you will not be formally detained. I ask that you comply and meet with authorities when we reach port. Can I count on you to do so?"

"Well, yes, you can." "Okay, fine, Chad, you'll be contacted just before we dock. Meanwhile, all is now as it was." Easy for him to say, I thought.

Yes, and as I walked back to my room my anxiety level seemed to be on the rise. Ah, but why worry? I still hadn't been arrested, and the USA was a long way back. Extradition and all that other baloney could take years. I had money!

I sat myself down and tried to get my mind on something else. I figured I'd give it some thought later. Some comedy, yeah. I flicked through the channels. Ah, my favorite Martian beer and potato chips should hit the spot. A couple more TV shows and I was as good as new.

I felt like calling someone for dinner. Right, Sharon. "Hello?"

"Hello, Sharon, how about dinner tonight?"

"Fine, what time?"

"At six thirty."

"Okay, great," she said. "Order for me."

Two lobster dinner were soon on the table. Since she sat across from me, it was apparent to her that I wasn't in the best of moods. And when I was more joyful, I overdid it. Thoughts of what happened earlier that day were not the easiest to suppress.

"Is everything alright?" she asked. "You look a little worried or something."

"Yeah, I am, no real big thing though." So I went into getting an address on how I could keep in touch with her. I have to meet with some people when we reach port. I told her I didn't and couldn't talk about what was on my mind. Not right now anyway. "I understand," she said.

So we sat around a while, giving each other bits of histories. A little lite exercise, I thought, would help. "How about a game of ping-pong?" I asked her. "Let's go!" she said.

Three days afterward, we reached the port of Marseilles, France. I received a call to my cabin asking me to meet with police officials in room 426. From there, I went along with them to an international building. There, someone from the U.S Embassy gave me some help in finding an attorney.

He gave me a list of names of counselors that spoke English. I picked one named Ronald Mikun. He advised me to say as little as possible and he would find out all he could about my case and also accompany me to the bond hearing. At this hearing, they said I was charged with the theft of 1.5 million in fragrance oil. My bond was set at $200,000. It took a couple of hours for things to clear with the bank in Arizona.

I then checked into a hotel and had a dinner brought to my room. I then went out for a good long walk!

The next day, I thought I'd go out for dinner and then hit one of the nearby night spots, which may have been the same place.

The following day, about 2:00 p.m., I took a sightseeing tour, which went on for the next two weeks. I got a good look at things to about a fifty-mile radius. It gave me a good Idea how the French live.

What I have been reluctantly waiting for happened. I received a call from my lawyer. The next day, I went into see Ronald Mikun.

"Chad, things might or might not be to your liking. As far as I'm concerned, I pat myself on the back," he said. "They seem to be an impatient group, and I used that to our advantage. I worked out a plea bargain with three options for you. Before we get to them, let me say this. They believe they have quite a bit of evidence that you're the person that committed this theft. Here is a list of what they're going to let us look at. After looking at it, you decide if you want a trial." He gave out a little laugh. "Or you would rather select one of the options of the plea bargain that I arranged?

"Chad, they don't want to go through the hassle and expense of a trial. Now let's talk about the options: (1) if you still have the oil, return it, (2) if you don't have the oil, they will settle for $750,000, or (3) if you don't have the oil or the cash, then you plead guilty and serve five to seven years in prison. Now if you agree to either of the first two options, you will receive five years' probation but no actual jail time."

Ron then put copies of what he had just talked about, plus a few other papers, into a tradition manila envelope. "Chad, do yourself a favor," he said. "Don't say anything until you read all this over carefully. Then give me a call. We'll set up another appointment."

And so for the next week, I sporadically looked over all the papers. In a way, I regretted not becoming an attorney myself. It's amazing. How simple all this is when you have an interest of some kind in it. Ron Mikun did about thirty hours of work, and he was going to get nine grands.

Subconsciously, when I walked out of his office last week, I knew already what I was going to do. I took out a piece of paper and started it with two words: *Dear Sharon*.

I loved her and she loved me, and I sure am glad she had money. We went on to live just outside Sierra Vista, Arizona, where we have a small horse ranch. We have two children. Our biggest problem is to watch our diets.

I go bowling about once a week. Sharon has her share of social activities also. I contacted Matt and let him know he didn't need to be anxious. He moved down here and remarried. I visit with my family around holidays, and hey, we're happy.

I guess that's about all for now.

ABOUT THE AUTHOR

Something the author lives
by day to day
"Kutianski Law"
What can go right, will go right

Author Dan Olt's real name is Chester Kutianski, born in Chicago, Illinois, to parents John and Diane Kutianski on February 14, 1950. One of his earliest loving memories was kneeling at the side of his bed with his parents a few feet away in their cozy flat. They guided him through a short prayer on a Saturday night. He has two older siblings, brother Joseph and sister Sophie. They grew up in a polished neighborhood and attended St. John of God Catholic School. Yes, this this is where he learned the discipline that taught him to accomplish anything he set his mind to do. His environment made staying on the straight and narrow a little swervy at times, but his belief in a higher power gave him the grace and fortitude to do. As with any young man, he sought adventure and, to this day, questions why we have wars. He waited to be drafted. After his two years in the army, he attended Daley College and received an associate of arts degree in liberal arts as he planned then worked as a machine shop quality control inspector. Currenly, Chester attends church on Sundays and is a firm believer in the hereafter and looks forward being with the Lord, family, and all of God's creation. He sends literature on research he has done to colleges. He has done natural ways of weight maintenance and enjoys life's blessings with family and friends. God blesses all of us.

CPSIA information can be obtained
at www.ICGtesting.com
Printed in the USA
BVHW032301240919
559315BV00001B/49/P